to John
Happy Christmas
Hong Kong

CW00968280

Cantonese Culture

Aspects of life in modern Hong Kong

and Southeast Asia

by

Shirley C. Ingram
&
Rebecca S.Y. Ng

Published in 1995 by Asia 2000 Ltd
1101–02 Seabird House
22–28 Wyndham St, Central
Hong Kong

ISBN 962 7160 37 7

First published in 1983
by Rebecca S.Y. Ng and Shirley C. Ingram
Second edition published in 1989 by Asia 2000 Ltd
Reprinted 1992
Third edition 1995

Printed in Hong Kong by Regal Printing

Preface

Living in Hong Kong has been a very exciting and enchanting experience. Often people, of a culture different from one's own, do not respond or react as expected. It is fascinating trying to understand and determine why they respond and react as they do. It is because of this fascination, and great desire to understand the people around me, that I have worked with one of my former language teachers, Mrs Rebecca S.Y. Ng, in writing this material. We have been very frank and open with each other; she in sharing her culture, and I in bluntly asking questions, as I sought to understand her culture.

This book was written with the hope that it will bring a deeper understanding of the everyday culture and customs of Cantonese people living in Hong Kong and other cities in Asia to its readers. It is especially hoped that it will help foreigners to more quickly and smoothly adapt to life here.

SHIRLEY C. INGRAM

Contents

Introduction

Hong Kong is not only a complex blend of Eastern and Western cultures; it is also made up of peoples from all areas of China, a vast country with many variations of culture and customs. Since Hong Kong is located on the southern coast of China, this discussion will basically reflect customs of the Cantonese, originally from Guangdong province. This effort to discuss Cantonese culture is only a general overview.

Topics covered in this book are ordinary things that happen in everyday life, from birth to marriage to death. These are approached from a viewpoint of trying to help the newcomer to have a basic understanding of the culture, and to know how to relate to people and situations. Of course, it would be impossible to cover all the customs of such a rich culture, but we have tried to cover most of those that might be confronted in everyday life.

Invited out to eat

Eating out is one of the most popular pastimes in Hong Kong. Restaurants are a popular meeting place for both social and business functions. A group eating together in a restaurant might range in number from two to two hundred, or more.

When invited to tea (a typical Chinese lunch) or an evening meal in a restaurant, a hostess gift is not generally given. However, if the guest knows ahead of time that there is a special reason for the invitation, such as a birthday, then a gift is given to the honoree.

In most circumstances, the guest should let the host order the food. Even if the host asks the guest what he would like to eat, the guest should be polite and not make requests, but eat whatever the host orders. Exceptions to this, of course, are made if the host and guest are very close friends or relatives. Then the guest can feel free to say if he does not eat certain things, or if there is something he especially would like to have.

Usually when invited for tea, *dim sum,* small pastries and meats that come around on carts, are chosen, and then some dishes of noodles and rice are ordered. If the guest is someone special, or the invitation is for a special reason, a few more expensive things might be chosen from the carts, such as roast pork or duck, to show special treatment to the guest.

When invited for a regular Chinese meal, which usually consists of several dishes of meats and vegetables, either to be eaten along with rice, or fried rice and noodles served at the end of the meal, the same general rules apply. The host orders the food. If the food seems sparse, the guests should just eat what is there. Even if the host asks if more is needed, the guests should politely say no. If the host's budget allows, and he sees that more food is really needed, he will insist on ordering more.

As to table manners, the guests should wait for the host to take up his chopsticks to start eating. Usually only a small portion is taken from the serving dish to the individual bowl at one time. This allows everyone an equal chance to share in the food. Sometimes the host may put a larger portion in the guests' bowls, but the guest, when helping himself, should take only a small amount each time.

If the table is large, and it is difficult to reach food on the other side, then usually the guest eats more of what is near him, occasionally reaching across the table. It is considered rude to stand up to reach across the table. The host should be considerate, and at least once during the meal, switch the dishes of food around to opposite sides of the table. If there is a turn-table in the middle, then the guests can feel free to spin it so they can get what they want.

At an informal meal, when time comes to pay, usually there is a wrangle over who gets to pay the bill. The one who originally invited should insist on paying the bill, and can say something to the guest like, "It will be your turn next time."

If there is no special reason for the dinner invitation, and the guest wishes, he can give lucky money to the host's children. Or, if the children will be present at the dinner, he can buy toys for the children; something that they can play with while the adults are eating and talking. If the host is an elderly person, lucky money can be presented to him in a red envelope, no matter if it is a special occasion or not.

Table manners

It is often difficult for the newcomer to Chinese culture to determine the appropriate etiquette for eating a Chinese meal. There are most definite dos and don'ts, just as there are in eating a Western meal.

When the meal is started and the first dish arrives, the guests wait for the host to begin. If it is a big dinner with many tables, quite often the chief host has assigned a person to host each table, so the guests should wait for their host to take the lead. If there is no assigned host, then someone will take the lead. Quite often the host will pick up his tea, soft drink, or wine, and everyone follows, drinking a toast to each dish before starting. Then the host will take up his chopsticks, and everyone follows his lead in taking food from the dish. Oftentimes the host will be more casual, and

at the beginning of the meal he will just tell everyone to help themselves, and there will be no more ceremony, the guests just eat together in a very informal way.

A piece of food that is nearest should be chosen from the serving dish, never reaching further to choose a better piece. When a piece of food has been handled with one's chopsticks, it must be taken; never change to another piece. If the food is hard to handle, it is perfectly all right to use the spoon to assist in getting it.

With a Chinese meal several dishes of sauce are served, and it is difficult to know which sauce is to be eaten with which kind of food. It is perfectly all right not to use the sauces, but these sauces are usually very delicious, and one can ask another person which sauces should be used with which foods. Sometimes the proper sauce is brought at the same time as the dish of food. A piece of food is usually dipped into the sauce; however, after a piece of food has been bitten on, it should not be dipped into the sauce. The spoon or chopsticks can be used to dip a little of the sauce onto the food.

It is just as impolite in Chinese culture as it is in Western culture to make noises with the mouth while drinking tea or eating food. Also, it is considered rude to talk with food in the mouth, or to chew with the mouth open.

Learning to eat with chopsticks takes practice, and especially handling food with bones in it. The bones may be removed from the mouth with the help of chopsticks, or the head may be bent down to let the bone fall from the mouth onto the bone dish. Sometimes in restaurants, especially at lunch time, there are no bone dishes, and the bones may be piled neatly at the side of the bowl.

The dishes of food are not passed around the table. They are placed in the middle of the table, and each person reaches to get a little as he wants it. A large portion is never taken at one time, allowing the food to be equally shared by all. Many times the host will be helpful in serving food, especially to a newcomer. There should be an extra pair of chopsticks placed in the middle, or on one side, of the table for this purpose. If there is not, the host will use the chopsticks of the person he is serving, or use his own, sometimes turning his chopsticks around to use the ends that have not been used to eat with. This is a way of showing concern and care, and should be accepted with graciousness. If a person has had enough of a particular food, he may graciously refuse by lightly placing his hand over his bowl.

The last piece of food is never taken from the dish, as the host will think his guests have not had enough, and will order more. Even if the host tries to insist that his guest take some, the guest should insist that he has had enough, so the host will not feel he has to order more. Of course, in situations where the guest and host have a very familiar relationship, this is not necessary. One might insist that the other finish the food on the dish, so that it is not wasted.

Chinese people do not use their hands for eating anything, not even chicken or shrimp. The only exception is for shrimp which have been boiled or steamed. Most shrimp have been stir-fried. In the beginning, the newcomer might feel that he is wasting food that cannot be eaten off the bone, but very soon he will become adept at using the chopsticks, and find that it is quite easy to eat most things with them.

Visiting homes

Visiting friends and relatives

When visiting in homes, Chinese people almost always carry a hostess gift; an exception might be when they visit a very close friend or relative. However, it depends on the individual person's custom. The gifts are usually food items, such as candy, cookies, fruit, bottles of fruit drink mix, or cakes from a bakery. These are accepted with thanks, but not opened in the presence of the guest (as is the usual custom of receiving gifts among Chinese people).

Immediately after a guest enters a home, the hostess will serve the guest a drink, usually tea; however, if the weather is hot, it may be something cold, such as a soft drink. If the guest has brought a hostess gift of something like cake or

fruit, and the hostess has nothing else prepared to serve, the cake or fruit can be served as a refreshment for all to enjoy together.

The length of a visit can vary greatly. It may be for half an hour, or it might be all day. If it is for all day, the idea is usually to play mah-jong or some other game. If the guest stays until meal time, the hostess will insist that the guest stay for the meal. The meal may be quite simple. The hostess might go out to buy some roast meat and other things that can be prepared quickly.

Visiting newly-weds

It is a custom to visit newly married couples about a week after they return from their honeymoon. If they do not go on a honeymoon, at least a week should go by after the wedding before friends start to visit. The purpose is to see the wedding pictures and their new home. Usually a hostess gift is taken to the new couple, just as when visiting at anytime in a home; a wedding gift would have been given when they were married. However, if it is known that there is a certain item that the couple needs for the home, this can be given instead of the usual cookies or candy.

The couple will show their wedding pictures, and maybe offer a few to the visitor, especially poses that include the visitor.

Visiting in a new home

It is also customary to visit and take a gift to a family who has just moved into a new home they have bought. It is not a general custom to give a gift if it is just a move from one rented place to another, because a person might move many times.

A usual type of gift for the home is a picture, vase, figurine, or other decorative item. However, if it is a close friend or relative, it is good to ask them what items are needed. For immediate family members, items such as a vacuum cleaner, oven, or lamp are usual gifts.

Often when a family buys a new home, they will invite friends and relatives to their home for a meal. Perhaps they will invite the wife's family first, and then the husband's family. Then they might invite different groups of friends, in turn. In this way their friends will have a chance to see the new home. If a gift for the new home has not already been given, it is appropriate to take one at this time.

However, sometimes a big meal will be held at a restaurant, and all friends and relatives will be invited at the same time. In this case, the guests may go to see the new home before going to the restaurant.

Visiting sick people

When visiting sick people, usually gifts of fruit, fruit juice, or a box of cookies are taken. Flowers are not taken, since they are used for funerals and in ancestral worship; therefore, traditionally, flowers are associated with death. Of course, in modern society, with the Western influence, there

are exceptions to this. If a family is quite West-
ernised, it probably would be quite acceptable to
take flowers. Also, many Christians reject the idea
that flowers are just for the dead, and appreciate
the cheerfulness that fresh flowers bring to the
sick room. However, if there is any doubt as to
the thinking of the sick person, it is better not to
take flowers. In general, it is best to take food
items; even if the sick person cannot eat them, the
family members can.

There are many people who are superstitious
and think that sick people should not be visited
at night. If a person is visited at night it shows
that the person is so ill that since there was not
time to visit during the day, time must be taken
to visit at night, since the sick person does not
have much time left. However, now, when most
people must work all day, and many hospitals
allow evening visiting, this custom has, for the
most part, been dropped.

When visiting sick people, of course words of
cheer and comfort should be said to them. Family
members might ask for a recommendation of a
better doctor. According to Chinese custom, a
doctor should never be recommended, since the
responsibility for the person's life is at stake. Of
course, if the family is seriously looking for a good
specialist in a certain field of medicine, and a
well-recognised one is known, it would not be
wrong to share this information with them.

When a sick person is visited and a gift is taken, the sick person, or family members, will give a red envelope of lucky money to the visitor. This is a means of saying thank you, and the amount of money varies, from twenty or so dollars, depending mostly on the family's financial circumstances. (This custom, however, has been dropped by many families today.)

There are occasions when money is given to a sick person, rather than food items. Sometimes it depends on the family's financial situation; or, it might depend on the relationship. For instance, if it is a relative of a relative (such as a sister's in-law), then money can be given to the sister with the request that she buy something the sick person needs. Also, a group, such as a church organisation, might put their money together and give it to the sick person to use as needed. Usually it is given with the explanation that the group does not know what the sick person can eat. Then, of course, the money can be used as needed.

Other courtesies

This chapter covers several topics, important but too brief for separate chapters.

Names

A lady always uses her whole name as given to her at birth; she never drops her maiden name. She adds on her husband's surname before her own. The name then reads: husband's surname, own surname, and given name (which usually consists of two words). However, most ladies, when asked their name, only give their own name, and must be asked their husband's name before it is given. Even if they know this is her husband's surname, they would assume that her maiden surname is the same as her husband's. Even the identity card or passport seldom includes the husband's surname.

It is always proper to address a person by their full name. In close relationships shorter names may be used (one part of the name), but even parents often address their children by their full name, including surname. Among adults it is quite customary to address each other as Mister or Mrs, even among good friends.

Gifts

When a gift is given, it is never opened in front of the giver. It is set aside and will be opened after the giver has left. The only exceptions to this is when the giver asks the receiver to open it. When a gift is given by a group to an individual they might ask the person to open it, so that all of the group can see it. Also, if the giver knows Western culture, and the receiver is a Westerner, they might tell the person he may open it

Relatives

Chinese have very specific terms for relatives, and there are so many that the Westerner finds them very difficult to learn; indeed they can be confusing even for Chinese people. For instance, if they speak of a brother, you know immediately if the brother is older or younger than the person speaking. If the person is speaking of an uncle, you know which parent's brother it is, and if the uncle is older or younger than the parent. For each relative the term is so specific that there is never a need to explain relationships.

Eating restrictions

As a Western person involves himself in Chinese culture, he soon becomes aware that there are unique ideas towards eating.

Often a Chinese person refuses to eat something because it will cause "hot air", or it is "cool". There seems to be no equivalent in the English language, but it means that the food will have some bad effect on the person. The effect can be anything, including indigestion, pimples, or sore (or scratchy) throat. So many more foods seem to effect a Chinese person in so many more ways than they do a Westerner. Whether these effects are because of a chemical difference in the make-up of the body, or are due to habits they have been taught while growing up, remains a question.

Also, there are many occasions when people either must eat certain things, or cannot eat others. For instance, if a person is sick he must have certain soups, but certainly cannot have anything cold. After surgery a person cannot eat beef, goose, or eggs, as it is believed they might cause the incision to get infected.

These are only examples of the unique eating habits found in Chinese culture. There are many, many more.

Jade

Top quality jade is rare, and is, therefore, expensive. Chinese people especially like jade not only for its beautiful colour, but because good jade represents status and wealth.

Chinese believe that jade has protective value. If a child wears a piece of jade (pendant or bracelet), he is protected from getting sick or getting hurt. Also, if a child has something happen to him that might cause him to have nightmares, such as an accident or other frightening experience, a piece of jade can be boiled in water, and then the water given to the child to drink. This is believed to prevent nightmares. Older people particularly believe this.

To give a gift of jade is to give a very special and meaningful gift. It is not given as a general gift, but only to very close relatives or friends, such as a daughter or daughter-in-law as a wedding gift, or a new-born child or grandchild.

There are many colours of jade, but most ranges in colour from white to many shades of green, with a wide range in value. It is very difficult to distinguish between good and poor qualities, and even an experienced person will not trust his eyes to judge quality.

Festivals

Most Chinese festivals are celebrated according to a lunar calendar of twelve months of 29 or 30 days, with a thirteenth month added every second or third year to bring it back into step with the seasons. The first of each month is a new moon, the full moon is about the fifteenth. Lunar New Year falls between late January and late February in the Western solar calendar.

New Year

Every Chinese household begins to prepare for the festivities of the New Year in the last month of the lunar year. The home must have a special cleaning before the new year begins, and often it will even be given a fresh coat of paint. Traditionally, everyone wears new clothes and shoes during

the New Year's celebration, so shopping must be done for this.

According to Buddhist custom, on the twenty-third day of the twelfth lunar month the kitchen god returns to heaven to rest. So, on this day the god must be worshipped and thanked for watching over the kitchen for the past year. A picture of the kitchen god hangs in the kitchen, and on this day they will stick a piece of candy on its mouth. The idea is to sweeten its talk, so that when it goes to heaven it will only tell good things about the family, and nothing bad, so the gods will be pleased and bless the family. That evening the family will have special foods, including chicken and roast pork, to serve and worship the kitchen god. Then the family will have a feast together and eat the food. The kitchen god will then be burned, and a new one hung up.

Sometimes a family will have a special service of thanksgiving during the last month of the lunar year. For instance, if a couple has prayed for and gotten a long-awaited child, or prayer for the healing of a very sick person has been answered, they will hold a service called a "gold pig", because they will buy a whole roasted pig and offer it to the gods. After they have used it to worship and thank the gods, they will cut it up and share it with family and friends. Chinese Christians have borrowed this idea; though they do not wait until the end of the year. A Christian will often give a special contribution to the church, and sometimes invite friends to share a meal with them, after God has granted a special blessing to them.

Just before New Year the price of food goes up daily, so all food items will be bought as early as possible. First, non-perishable foods will be bought, such as dried mushrooms and shrimp, flour and rice. The traditional "year" cake will be bought, and turnip root cake will be made. Many families will fry special dumplings. Also for the first five days (or for some people, fifteen days) of the new year a knife will not be used. So, much food has to be prepared in advance. Today, this custom is seldom adhered to.

On New Year's Eve everyone must go to the parents' home for the big family meal together. (In Chinese custom the wife becomes a part of her husband's family, so they naturally go to his parents' home.) However, in the modern situation, where many people will work on New Year's Eve, a family often chooses another time to have their big dinner together. It might be several days before New Year, or it might be on New Year's Day. But, almost every family will find a time to celebrate the New Year together. Of course, it will be a very special meal which will include mushrooms; *fat choy,* a stringy vegetable that looks like hair, because the words sound like *fat choy,* prosperity; pig's feet, which represents being lucky in winning money in gambling; pig's tongue, which represents everything will go smoothly; and many other special foods. The food must be plentiful and some must be left over for the next day, as superstition says that this shows that the New Year is starting off with plenty, and there will be plenty all year.

On New Year's Eve, boys (never girls) from poorer families might go from door to door with red papers, which have the words "wealth god" written on them. They will knock on the door and say the wealth god has come. The family will take one of the red papers, stick it on their door, and give lucky money to the boys. The wealth god is supposed to bring prosperity to the family in the new year. (Christians usually do not participate in this practice.)

It is customary not to sleep on New Year's Eve. At exactly midnight the gods and ancestors must be worshipped. After worshipping the gods and ancestors all the children, from the oldest to youngest, will, in turn, serve tea and bow to the parents, thanking them for taking care of them during the past year. If a child is married, the child and his mate will serve the tea together. The parents will give lucky money to the children in turn. Then they will play cards or other games until morning, when the children will again serve tea to the parents and other elders, and wish them good health and a happy new year. The parents will, in turn, give lucky money to the children again.

Another custom for New Year's Eve is to go to the flower market. The flower markets are set up about two weeks before New Year. Not many people go to buy flowers so early, as they will die before New Year. But people go to buy the peach trees and orange trees. Earlier, one can have a good selection to choose from, but they are very expensive. On New Year's Eve the prices are much lower. After the family has dinner, they might play cards or watch television, and then go the flower market after midnight, when the flowers are very cheap. After 2 AM they are even cheaper, because the vendors need to sell them all; the next day nobody will want to buy flowers.

People especially like to buy peach trees and small sour-orange trees. Once a person buys one, they must buy one every year, or else they will have bad luck. The more fruit or flowers the better the buyer's luck will be during the coming year. Also, the flowers must open by New Year's Day, or else their luck will not be good. If a person cannot afford the orange or peach trees, there are many other kinds of flowers to buy. Business people feel they must buy the peach and orange trees. In the past the flower markets only had plants and flowers to sell, but today they have toys, foods, and many other things. For many people who work and have no time to shop, this provides opportunity to buy hostess gifts they will need when they go visiting during the New Year.

On the first day of the New Year, if the family is Buddhist, they are not supposed to eat meat. However, this custom has been modified, and some people will do without meat only for the noon meal, but will eat meat in the evening.

Also, on the first day of the New Year, most families stay at home, because they have slept very little, if any, on New Year's Eve.

Another custom is not to sweep the floor on the first day, because it symbolises sweeping away money. If the house is very dirty and must be swept, it must be swept towards the inside of the house, not towards the door, so as to keep money coming into, not out of, the house.

The noon meal on the second day of the New Year is called "starting of the year dinner". This signifies that the New Year has begun. This meal is usually quite early in the day, around 10 AM. After this the families start visiting relatives to wish them a happy new year. There is a protocol — the younger must visit their elders, whether it is the older generation, or older brothers and sisters. A hostess gift is always taken when visiting at New Year; originally these were gifts of fruit or homemade steamed cakes. Nowadays it is fruit or boxes of candy or cookies. Married people must carry many of the red envelopes of lucky money to give to children and unmarried relatives.

At New Year, when people see each other, they have special greetings. The most common is *"Kung Hei Fat Choy"*, which means congratulations and prosperity. Other greetings include, "Good health", "Congratulations and have more children", (said to young married people), "Hope you get a promotion", (said to working people) and "Hope you make progress" (said to students). When visitors arrive at a home, the first thing the hostess does is to pour a cup of tea for the guests. Of course, the usual New Year snacks are served: steamed cake, fried dumplings, preserved fruits, and melon seeds. That day it is not necessary to eat another meal, because food is eaten at each home visited. However, often the day is ended by eating dinner with close relatives, such as a sister or brother.

Traditionally, there was no celebrating on the third day of the year. Everyone was so tired, and it was easy to get into arguments, so everyone stayed home to rest. Celebrations began again on the fourth day. In the past, celebrations of the New Year sometimes lasted a month. In rural settings with slow, or no, transportation, it took a long time to go to visit friends and relatives, and the length of time was stretched out to facilitate being able to visit everyone.

In Hong Kong the situation is different. Public holidays are only three days, and if friends and relatives are not visited on these days, then there is no opportunity. Most people start back to work on the fourth day. So, now visiting is done on the first and third days as well.

Some larger families set a certain time for all of them to get together at the oldest family member's home instead of visiting each others' homes. All of the married people give lucky money to all of the children. Then they usually have dinner together. It is a very happy occasion for the family, and saves lots of time, especially in transportation.

Often, on the third day colleagues will get together at noon for tea in a restaurant. This is also to save time, as then they do not need to visit in each others' homes.

After people return to work, they still will go to visit, in the evening or on weekends, those who they could not get around to visiting during the public holidays.

In busy Hong Kong people usually only visit very close relatives and friends. They might telephone others to let them know they are thinking of them.

All businesses and factories will take a holiday for New Year, even though they might take none during the rest of the year. If stores are open, it is because the owner keeps it open. The hired workers all get holidays, or special compensation.

In the past all restaurants also closed. In recent years many remain open, but they raise the prices of the food, and the ten percent service charge is raised to twenty. Because few people are at work at New Year, the restaurants are especially busy.

Many people join overseas tours at this time. For some factory workers it is the only holiday they have during the year; but they may take as many as fifteen days at this time.

One thing that every home must have at New Year is the box of sweets for people to eat when they come to visit. Traditionally, this consisted of dried lotus seeds, coconut strips, melon strips, and melon seeds. However, today many younger families do not like to eat these very much, so they buy a couple of kinds of the traditional sweets, and then some other things, such as chocolates and other candies to serve to the guests.

In some homes a lucky money envelope is placed in this dish of candy by the hostess. If the guest sees that the box has a red envelope there, the guest then puts an envelope of lucky money in the box. This is just a symbol to show that the guest wishes the family good luck, and usually only a small amount of money is in the envelope.

If there is a servant in the home who serves tea, lucky money should be given to the servant by the guest.

Homes customarily have fresh flowers at New Year, even if they usually do not at other times. This is just for beauty; there is no special significance.

Before New Year's Day, gifts are given to older immediate family members, and business people give gifts to customers. The most common gifts are dried sausages, dried ducks, fresh fruit, and wine. The reason is that they are expensive treats that do not have to be refrigerated. After New Year every household has sausages, and if company comes unexpectedly, they can be quickly prepared.

Mid-Autumn festival

This festival is on the fifteenth day of the eighth month of the lunar calendar. It is also called the Moon Festival.

There are several stories of this festival. One is that in China, during the Yun Dynasty, each family had to take in Mongolians to care for, at the ratio of one for each ten family members. But the people disliked Mongolians very much, so they were always plotting to kill them. At the time, there was a great fear of the plague, and the people would eat a certain kind of round cake that they thought would prevent it. Then one day someone got the idea that in each cake they would put a message saying which day they would kill all the Mongolians. The Mongolians could not read Chinese, so there was no fear that they would know. Also, since the ratio was ten Chinese to one Mongolian, this plan would be very easy to carry out. So, on the appointed day the people got rid of all the Mongolians in their midst. The cakes,

called moon cakes, are still eaten today at Moon Festival time.

Another story is that a long time ago, also during the Yun Dynasty, China had a war with Mongolia. China sent some people to that country as spies. After the spies found out when Mongolia was planning to attack China, they had to find a way to get the news to the emperor. Finally they thought of making a cake, writing the date of attack on a small piece of paper, putting it inside the cake, and sending the cake to the emperor. Then they asked someone to go by horse to deliver the cake as quickly as possible. The emperor thought it strange that a cake was so urgently sent to him. He cut it open immediately, and saw the piece of paper inside. He opened it and saw the date on it, and knew that this was the date that the Mongolians planned to attack his country. So they made a plan; they gathered all their soldiers together on that night

to take up their torches and go to war. As a result, they won the battle.

Besides eating moon cakes, lanterns are burned on this day. The lanterns represent the torches carried by the soldiers. Today the lanterns are in many shapes, such as animals, cars, and airplanes, as well as the usual lantern shape.

On the evening of the Mid-Autumn Festival most families gather together for a big dinner. They then go outdoors, usually to a park, for the children to light their lanterns and play. Later they eat moon cakes and fruit. Fruits are eaten to help digest the rich moon cakes, such as persimmons, star fruit, and pomelos, since these are in season at that time. Other customary snack foods eaten for this festival are boiled taro roots and chestnuts.

Some people also call this the time for "worshipping" the beautiful moon. They say there is a lady fairy in the moon. She will protect the people, so they must worship her. Also, there is a rabbit in the moon who helps the fairy by cutting wood for her.

Everyone must go out to see the moon. In crowded Hong Kong it is not easy to find a place for a family to sit out and enjoy the fresh air and the beauty of the full-moon night. Families go out with their food, tablecloths, radios, lanterns, and battery-operated lights, and very early in the evening all space is filled. This is usually true for both the nights before and after the actual date of the festival, even in all of the New Territories, especially if a car is driven and a parking space is needed. Some people even rent boats and go out on the water to celebrate.

Gifts of moon cakes and fruit are given on this occasion to the older generation. Mooncakes are given because they are round in shape, and symbolise never-ending union. Fresh fruit represents life. Business people also give gifts of moon cakes, fruit, and wine to their customers at this time.

Moon cakes are quite expensive, and businesses have come up with a way of earning more money by selling them on installment plan. However, the money is paid in advance; payments made this year are for next year's cakes. But, for the customer it is actually cheaper to buy on the installment plan. For example, for ten boxes, payments of $75 per month are paid for twelve months. This is $90 per box, but if bought at the time of the Mid-Autumn Festival, they might be $100 per box.

At this festival lucky money is also given. It is given by those who receive a gift to those who give, and also to people such as garbage collectors and building guards, to show appreciation for their services.

Dragon Boat festival

The story of this festival is that a long time ago, during the Cho Kwok time, there was a patriotic poet, whose name was Wat Yun. He loved his country very much. However, the emperor of China at that time was not very clear of mind, and was influenced by a certain official. He told the emperor that Wat Yun was deceiving him, that he actually did not want to be helpful, but that he wanted to harm him. So, the emperor sent Wat Yun off to the border area, where nobody lived. There he had to live a hard life off of the land.

Wat Yun was very unhappy; he was so loyal to his country, and yet the emperor did not believe him. So, he wrote a poem. This poem was his thoughts, written from his heart to the emperor. He told the emperor that he had been tricked by this deceitful person, and he knew this was the only reason the emperor would do such a thing as to send him away. He believed that in the future the emperor would understand.

After he wrote the poem, on the fifth day of the fifth month of the lunar year, he went to the river and jumped in and drowned himself. Many people went in boats to look for him. They beat drums to frighten the fish away so they would not eat Wat Yun's body. They also wrapped rice and food in bamboo leaves and dumped it in the river, hoping the fish would eat this instead, so that they would be able to find it.

In the end, the emperor realised his error, but it was already too late. Wat Yun was dead. And that is why we have the Dragon Boat Festival, to commemorate Wat Yun and his love for his country.

Today, this festival is celebrated by eating glutinous rice wrapped in bamboo leaves, and racing dragon boats. Originally it was celebrated just by riding in boats, but gradually people started racing. Drums are also beaten, and nowadays this is so the oarsmen can row to the rhythm of the drums.

There are several kinds of glutinous rice dumplings. Some are made with meat and mushrooms, some with peanuts, and some are sweet with red beans. They are wrapped with bamboo leaves in the shape of a small pillow.

Some people believe that the morning of that day is an auspicious time. For instance, if a person is sick and he takes a special medicine on that morning, he will get well. Also, if a person with a skin disease goes to a river or ocean on that morning and immerses in the water his skin will get well very quickly. They think that Wat Yun was holy, and that the waters of the oceans and rivers become holy on that day.

At this festival, gifts of glutinous rice dumplings are given to family members, especially the older generation. If a woman knows how to make them herself, she might even make them to give to the children of family members. Nowadays, most people do not make them at home, but buy them. Noodle restaurants and many other places sell them. They can be bought early and put in the refrigerator. On the day of the festival usually plain congee and glutinous rice dumplings are eaten, a very simple meal. The dumplings can be reheated by boiling for about thirty minutes. The leaves are wrapped very securely, so there is no fear of water getting into the dumpling.

Winter festival

This festival is on December 22, according to the solar calendar, and not the lunar, as other Chinese festival dates are chosen. The reason is that it is the shortest day of the year, and it is always on the same date by the solar calendar, but would always be different by the lunar calendar. All factories close for the day, and also some offices, schools, and other businesses will close, some only for the afternoon.

In the past Chinese considered this festival as important as New Year. They visited each other, and celebrated much in the same way as New Year. Today it is only a family celebration, and restaurants and stores close early in order for families to be together. Everyone must eat round dumplings, as the round shape symbolises a never-ending relationship.

There is no special significance to this festival, it is just a big family get-together. The married children go to the home of the man's parents to eat, usually, but if there are small children, then perhaps, for convenience' sake, the meal will be held at the home of a son who has small children. This is a very simple occasion, and no gifts or lucky money are given.

SPECIAL FESTIVALS FOR WORSHIPPING ANCESTORS

Ching Ming

This festival is traditionally for worship of ancestors at the grave site; however, there is a great difference in the way that Christians and Buddhists celebrate this day.

For Christians it is a simple remembrance of the ancestors. They place flowers on the grave and clean the grave. They can go on the day of the festival, or choose another convenient day, before or after. They might have a prayer together as a family, but it will be for the living family members, not for the dead.

For Buddhists, it is quite different. For instance, for the first few years after a person's death, the family must go to the grave on the exact day of Ching Ming. After that they may go on any day near the date. When Buddhists go to worship at the grave they will take such things as chicken, roast pork, steamed bread pastries, rice, wine, incense, candles, and paper money and clothes. (The money and clothes can be bought in the shops where incense and candles are sold.) The food is for the spirit to eat, and the other items are for worshipping the spirit of the ancestor. Some people also place fresh flowers on the grave, and some people burn firecrackers. Then, the family will usually have a picnic at the graveside, and eat the food that has been offered to the spirit.

Ancestors are worshipped for several generations, both at the graveside and in the home. A
plaque with the names is placed in a special place
in the home, which is called the "god place", or
altar. On special occasions the family will worship
the ancestors at the altar.

Chung Yeung

This festival is also known as Chung Kau (*kau*
means nine) because the festival is on the ninth
day of the ninth month of the lunar year.

The original meaning of this festival was not
to worship ancestors, but simply to climb a
mountain. The story is that an emperor was
attacked by an enemy, and had to flee from the
palace. The emperor and his entourage put on
clothes like farmers, so people would not recog-
nise them. They gathered up some money and
food and wrapped it in cloth and went as refugees
to the mountains. The war went on for a long
time before they finally conquered the enemies
and were able to return to the palace.

So, in remembrance of this occasion people
started to climb mountains each year on that date,
just for an outing and picnic.

Eventually, people started thinking that since
they were going up the mountain anyway, they
might as well clean the graves and worship their
ancestors. (Traditionally, graves are on mountains.) So, this became the second day in the year
for ancestor worship.

Some people feel that if a person has not been dead very long, they should worship him at both festivals. However, Ching Ming is the most important of the two, and if a family chooses to go only once a year, it will be at Ching Ming. In Hong Kong it is very noticeable that more people go at Ching Ming than Chung Yeung, as the traffic is much heavier on the roads.

Actually, from a practical standpoint, Ching Ming and Chung Yeung Festivals are a time to clean up the graves. Grass and weeds are cut and pulled away so the grave can be seen. Also, if need be, the name on the stone is repainted. So, when someone says he is going to "sweep the grave", this is actually what he will do.

Lucky Money

Money placed in special red envelopes, *lai see,* and given as gifts is known as lucky money. It is a very prominent part of Chinese culture; and is given as a gift on many occasions.

At Lunar New Year it is given by married people to their own children, and to all unmarried children of relatives and friends. If a person goes to a friend's home to visit during the days of the celebration of the New Year, and there is someone else visiting in the home who has children, even though he does not know them, he must also give lucky money to these children, though less than that given to friends and relatives. If a person does not give lucky money, people will say, "Oh, this person does not have lucky money." Saying this is supposed to bring bad luck to the person.

The amount of lucky money given, of course, depends on the family's financial situation. Some people will put $50, $100, or even $500 in each envelope. But this is rare; usually large amounts are only given to one's own children or *kai* children. The average amount given is $20.

The customs of north and south China are different regarding giving lucky money. In the north married couples give one envelope together. In the south a couple gives two envelopes, one from each of them. If only one is given from a married person from southern China, it is because the spouse has died. In the case of a couple giving two envelopes, less money is put in each envelope than if the couple gives one envelope together. For instance, if a couple gives one envelope they might put in $20, whereas, if they each give an envelope they would only put $10 in each one.

The amounts given are different depending on closeness of relationship, so envelopes with different amounts must be prepared. Nieces and nephews might be given $50, friends' children $20, and children of casual acquaintances $10.

When visiting in homes at New Year, hostess gifts are taken, and lucky money is given in return for the gift. Also, lucky money is given in return for any gift given for festivals, weddings, birthdays, or to a sick person. For ordinary visits to homes when hostess gifts are taken, no lucky money is given.

If invited to a home to eat, and a servant cooks the meal, lucky money should be given to the servant. At New Year, even if a meal is not eaten in the home, but the servant serves tea, lucky money should be given to her. More money is given when a meal is served than when only tea is served.

Lucky money is also given to building guards, caretakers, and garbage collectors. At present the usual amount to give is $10 or $20, and this is given especially at New Year and the Mid-Autumn Festival.

Some Chinese people always carry *lai see* with them. For instance, a person might be invited to dinner without being told it is someone's birthday. If after arriving he realises it is someone's birthday, he can then put some money in the envelope and give it to the honoree.

When out-of-colony relatives or friends come to visit, if it is not convenient to bring a gift, they often give lucky money instead. It is usually given to the children, but the parents know it is really a hostess gift.

Marriage

The Matchmaker

In traditional Chinese society, the matchmaker's role was to help get well-matched young people together to form a compatible marriage relationship. She would get pictures of both the young man and young woman of whom she wished to match. In turn, she would take the pictures of the young people to the prospective in-laws to see. As the families, in turn, viewed the pictures, the matchmaker would tell all the virtues of the young person to the prospective in-laws. The matchmaker would do her best in making a good and successful match, because her livelihood depended on it.

The role of the official, paid, matchmaker still exists. However, there are some who claim to help find wives for men, such as the ones who bring in girls from Thailand. In most cases this is a racket; the girl comes and manages to get all the man's money from him through deception, and then returns home. However, sometimes a man who is approaching middle age and still has not found a wife, is successful in finding a wife through a matchmaker.

There is another method of matchmaking that is still very common. When a boy and girl approach their parents with plans of marriage, often one of the parents will take them to a fortune teller to see if they are well-matched. (A fortune teller sign can be spotted on the streets of Hong Kong, just as in Western countries, by the palm-of-a-hand emblem.) First of all, they compare the year, date, and time of the couples' births, which should be compatible. If these do not match, the fortune teller will show them ways to match, such as adding, subtracting, or multiplying the numbers. The girl might be asked to take on a new name to make them compatible. Or, for instance, the fortune teller might tell the girl that even though the man she is planning to marry does not have money now, she is a lucky person, and she will bring good fortune to the marriage.

Engagement

Sometimes the engagement of couples will follow the pattern of Western culture, in that an engagement ring is given to the future bride by the future groom, and sometimes an engagement party or ceremony is held.

But, even if some patterns of Western culture are followed, usually many Chinese practices are maintained. The tendency is that Christian families do not follow the Chinese cultural practices to the extent that non-Christians follow them, the main reason being that there is much superstition involved. However, there are few families where both the bride's and groom's parents are Christian, and, since parents have heavy influence in how the wedding is carried out, in most cases many of the traditional customs are adhered to. Even if both families are Christian, many Chinese customs will probably be carried out.

In Chinese culture there is no engagement ceremony. The engagement of a couple becomes official at the time the dowry is given by the groom's family to the bride's family. This may take place from two weeks up to three months before the wedding. The dates for the engagement and wedding are set according to the lunar calendar. The almanac explains which days are auspicious, and dates will be chosen accordingly. The value of the dowry, of course, depends mainly upon how much the groom can afford.

The bride's mother represents her family in making a list of things she expects the dowry to contain, and sends it to the groom's family. If the groom's family feels it cannot fulfill the expectations, they will bargain with the bride's family to get the list down to a reasonable amount. The list will include expensive food items, such as dried mushrooms, dried abalone, dried scallops, dried shrimp, live chickens, pig's feet, wine, candies, fruits, and many other items.

There are two things the list must include. One is a pair of lotus roots, tied together with red string. The Cantonese word for lotus *lin ngau,* sounds like the word for connect, *lin,* and so the lotus roots tied together symbolise a lasting relationship. The other is four coconuts with the character meaning happiness written on them. The Cantonese words for coconut, *yeah tchee,* sound like the words for grandfather, *yeah,* and son, *tchee,* and symbolise that many generations will come from this union. The family will also ask for a number of gift cards for cakes (both Western and Chinese) and roast meats to pass out to their friends as a means of celebrating and announcing the wedding of their daughter. Some gold and money will also be requested. Shoes, or money to buy shoes, will be requested for the bride's younger, unmarried brothers. Also, pants, or money to buy pants, will be requested for older unmarried brothers and sisters of the bride. The items are delivered to the bride's home by a servant or relative of the groom, never by the groom's parents. The groom's family will make a celebration of this event, by asking relatives to come help them pack the items and get them ready to send. When the goods are delivered to the bride's family, the bride's family will return a portion of the goods to the groom's family, as a polite way of showing that they have been too generous, and need not have sent so much. Also, the bride's family will send two lucky money envelopes for the groom. One is for buying a suit, and the other for buying shoes.

The bride's family will then have a big dinner and invite their relatives and close friends. The groom's family will not be invited to this dinner.

It is the responsibility of the groom to provide housing for himself and his new bride. However, the bride's family will provide all the household goods for the new couple, except for the bed. The groom must buy the bed — if the bride's parents buy the bed it symbolises that nobody wants the daughter, and they had to buy it to convince someone to take her. The bride's parents will also give jewellery to her as a wedding gift. The amount they give depends on their financial situation, but even the poorest will do their best to give at least a small piece of gold jewellery to their daughter. Gold and precious stones will last forever, so it felt that such a gift must be given.

Wedding

The night before the wedding, a lady, one with many sons (having many sons means she will bring good luck), is invited to come to the bride and groom's new home to make their new bed and to prepare a dish of candied fruits for guests who come the next day to visit the new bride. This lady is an acquaintance of the family, usually a good friend or relative. There is no fee for this service, but she is given a packet of lucky money.

In the past, a professional in the field of wedding manners was hired for the wedding day. She was called the bride's assistant, and assisted the bride in all the formalities she must go through on her wedding day. She was usually over forty years old, and the usual fee for her was $40, plus

$2 for each table at the wedding feast, plus half of the lucky money the bride received from the wedding dinner guests. Nowadays, the bride may ask one of her friends to be her helper, *boon leung,* and she will be given a few hundred dollars in lucky money.

The night before the wedding, the groom, his best man, and other male friends would party the whole night, usually playing mah-jong. This custom is not always carried out today, as many grooms prefer to be rested for the busy wedding day.

The bride also gathers with her friends on the night before the wedding. (The traditional reason was that she would leave home and it would be a long time before she would return, so her friends

would take this last opportunity to visit her before she left.) A special lady, who is supposed to bring much good luck, is asked to come at a certain time to comb the bride's hair and to make up her face for the wedding day. With each stroke of the brush to the hair she intones "good luck" sayings. She also places flowers and jewellery in the hair, according to the bride's wishes. Customarily, the bride and her friends also did not sleep for the whole night, but this custom is not always carried out today.

Preparations are made for the next morning, when the bridegroom and his friends come to receive the bride. The bride cannot open the door; it must be opened by her bridal party. Her bridal party will bargain with the groom before they give the bride to him. They might start with a very high figure, such as $99,999.99. The number nine has the same sound in Cantonese as the word for "long time", and, of course, this has the implication that they will be married for a long time. They will bargain for a long time, and the bridal party will settle for a much lower amount, sometimes as little as $99.99. This money is given in a lucky money envelope, and is given to the bridal party as a whole, not as individual packets. After they receive the money, they then let the groom and his party in to receive the bride. At this time the bride and groom serve tea to the bride's parents and receive lucky money from her parents. The bride's family will invite them to eat.

What they eat depends upon their family traditions, and this has become more and more simple in recent years. Usually it is something like noodle soup, cakes, or other pastries.

Then both the bride's and groom's parties go to the groom's home to see his parents. The bride's parents do not go; however, brothers and sisters of the bride who are not married may go. The purpose of this trip to the groom's home is for the bride to officially meet the groom's parents. His parents sit very formally for this ritual of the wedding day. The bride's assistant helps her in this, preparing a cup of tea for the bride and groom to serve to his parents. This cup of tea must contain some sugar and two lotus seeds. The sugar represents a sweet relationship in the future, and the lotus seeds represent having a child in the coming year. The bride and groom kneel before his parents to serve the tea to them. At this time the groom's parents will present a gift to the bride. Usually it is an item of gold jewellery, and what they give depends upon what they can afford. They might give a necklace or a bracelet; if not, then a smaller item such as a ring. If they can afford it, they might even give diamonds. They will also present the bride and groom with a packet of lucky money.

After the parents, the bride and groom then go to the groom's older brothers and sisters to serve tea and receive their wedding gifts. These older brothers and sisters will also give jewellery to the bride.

Unless the family is Christian, the couple then go to worship the ancestors. The home has an ancestral tablet with the names of the ancestors listed on it. The couple bows before the tablet and burns incense to them. If the bride and groom are Christians, it is usually only required that they nod their heads in acknowledgment of the ancestors.

If the wedding is to take place in a church, it is at this time that the bride changes into the white wedding dress. If they are not getting married in a church, she will continue to wear her red Chinese wedding dress, and at this time she puts on all the jewellery she has received. She will not wear her jewellery to the church, but will wait until later to put it on, and wear it at the wedding feast. It is important that she wear it, out of respect for those who gave it, but special precautions must be taken so that thieves do not take advantage of the situation.

After the visit to the groom's home (or after the wedding, if it is at a church), the new couple must go to their new home, along with their wedding party. They must serve tea, and perhaps noodles, or other snacks. However, the snacks must be sweet. Even if noodles are served they will be sweet, and, perhaps, with eggs, but never with meat. They then must return to the girl's family's home for a visit. This is a custom left over from the past when it was not so easy for the bride to return to her home. So, on the third day they returned for the bride to visit her family. In today's situation, it is easy for the bride to go to visit her family, so it has become just a symbolic visit, and is carried out as a part of the wedding day activities. Then, at about five in the afternoon, it is time to go to the restaurant for the wedding feast.

The restaurant has a bride's room, and the bride goes immediately to this room to receive friends and relatives. After a while photographs begin to be taken, and every relative and friend wants to be sure to have a picture taken with the bride and groom. Many, many pictures are taken, and this is a long and tiring process for the bride and groom.

After the wedding feast starts, when the first two or three courses have been eaten, the bride and groom will then show respect to their guests for coming to the feast by drinking toasts to them. The bride's assistant or a staff member of the restaurant leads the wedding party from table to table to drink toasts to all of the guests. Each table of guests will stand as the wedding party approaches. The table of their own parents is always first, as they thank their parents for all they have done for them.

In the past there were two separate rounds of drinking cheers. The groom and bride separated, he went with his father and older brothers and the bride's father and older brothers, and wine was used to drink cheers to the guests. The bride went with her mother and older sisters and the groom's mother and older sisters, and they used tea to drink cheers to the guests. At present, the bride and groom usually join together in drinking cheers. As they go from table to table, their friends will tease them with remarks such as, "Be sure to invite us to the feast next year." The meaning, is, of course, to the feast for the celebration of the birth of their first child.

After drinking toasts, the bride goes to her room and changes from the wedding dress into another formal dress. By then it is about time for the feast to be finished, and the wedding party goes to stand at the door to speak to the guests as they leave.

After the guests have gone, the restaurant account must be settled. The restaurant gives a gift of a pair of chopsticks, a bowl, a dish, and a spoon to the bride and groom. On the chopsticks will be carved, in Chinese, "100 years of good unity". In return the bride and groom present a packet of lucky money to the restaurant staff. Then the bill for the feast is settled. Of course, a tip will be added to this amount. This is a very formal transaction, and during the process the restaurant staff will say many expressions of good fortune. During this procedure the bride and groom will give additional tips, five or more times. Then the staff will see the bride and groom to the door. In recent years this has been simplified, as the restaurant has a set time for closing, and the staff expects to get off work on time.

As to gifts for the bride and groom, most people give money, which is usually presented in the form of gift certificates. These can be bought at many banks. However, closer friends and relatives will give personal gifts. Usually the bride receives several gifts of gold jewellery. These may be given by individuals, or by groups. Also, more practical gifts are given, such as household items. A large group of friends might even go together to present the bride and groom with a refrigerator, or other large item. The wedding gift must be given on or before the wedding day, never after. If it is impossible to give the gift earlier, then later a gift can be given for the new home.

The wedding feast is quite an expense for the groom. Even though the couple receives quite a number of cash gifts, probably the most they can expect is eighty percent of the cost, and many times much less, depending on how many of the guests give personal gifts. The cost per table for a feast is general knowledge, and it is customary for the guests to give a cash gift of an amount that will cover the cost of their meal. It is easy to find out the appropriate amount to give by asking friends.

The bride's parents and the groom's parents do not include each other in most family affairs. However, they do have a special relationship, and at New Year and at the Moon Festival they send gifts to each others' homes as a token of this.

Position of elderly in the family

In Chinese families, elderly people retain a role of status and respect in the family; however, the role is quite different today than in the past. The oldest family member was the ruler of the family, respected and obeyed by all family members.

The extended family living together used to be the pattern of life. The oldest family member was the head, and made all decisions, small and large, including matters relating to finances. This held true in both the richest and poorest of families.

Children were taught from the time they were very young to never disagree with an elderly person, even if they knew he was wrong. Because they were raised in this atmosphere, no one ever thought of showing disrespect for his elders.

Decisions regarding children, grandchildren, or great grandchildren had to be approved by the head of the house. If a grandchild wanted to marry a certain person and his parents were in complete agreement, but the head of the house disapproved, he could not marry that person. Even if a person did not really love their elder, they would never show it; outwardly only love and respect was seen.

The extended family style of living is no longer common in Hong Kong. The main reason is that the housing facilities do not allow for it. The second reason is that the culture has mixed with

Western culture, and most people have come to realise that the extended family system has its problems. The thinking of two generations is quite different, and then, after children come and a third generation lives in the same house, there is an even greater gap in their thinking.

However, this is not to say that modern Chinese do not respect their elders, it is just that the way they show respect to their elders has changed. Also, Chinese people now speak their thoughts more freely, and if they disagree with something, they will speak out. Today, no matter whether it is to parents or grandparents, the younger generation can voice their opposition. Of course, this is usually done in a very polite way, explaining their reasons for opposing. There are some people who will just ignore, or even scold their elders; however, this is not considered acceptable behavior.

Sometimes when an older person feels he is being disrespected and mistreated, it is simply a lack of his understanding of the changing times. As an older person, he remembers the ways in which he showed respect for his elders, and he expects to be treated in the same way.

Also, in the individual family system, a couple has authority over their own family. If the older generation tries to maintain authority, problems arise. There are still situations under which three generations can live together quite peacefully. For instance, if the older person is able to take care of himself, and is also able to make a contribution to the household by helping with the children or other household chores, then the two generations might live together in peace. But, if there is interference by the older generation into the younger generation's affairs, then many problems can arise. The son is then caught in the middle, between his parents and his wife, and is in quite a difficult position.

Usually, if parents live with a daughter rather than a son, there are less problems, and they get along better. The parents feel they must be polite to the son-in-law, as they are guests in the house, and must do their part to make things run smoothly. If they live in a son's home, they feel that their son has an obligation to take care of them, and the daughter-in-law is obligated to serve them. No matter what they do to help, they feel they are under no obligation to do it, and are doing it as a favour.

Parents of today teach their children to respect their grandparents. They explain that the grandparents are much older and their thinking is different. The education they received was much different than what the child now gets, and society today is much different than when the grandparents were young. They also explain that it is not easy for old people to change their way of thinking. The young people are taught that if they have conflicts with the grandparents, they must treat them with respect and give explanations to them as to why they disagree.

If older people are sick, the younger generations, both children and grandchildren, feel a deep responsibility for taking care of them, both physically and financially. This responsibility is ingrained in the minds and hearts of Chinese people, and under normal circumstances they will not neglect their elders.

The old-age pension system of Hong Kong is weak, and the government support of old people is quite insufficient. So, when children grow up and start to work they are expected to help financially with the support of both parents and grandparents. It is the only means of security for old age.

Another problem is that there are not nearly enough homes for the aged in Hong Kong. However, Chinese, in general, do not like living in homes for the aged. Traditionally, Chinese liked to have many sons and daughters, so that when they were old they would have their children to take care of them. The parents would put all their efforts into raising and educating their children, almost as if an investment for their future, so the children could support them well. So, usually, the only people who went to homes for the aged were people with no children, nieces, or nephews to take care of them. It was their very last resort for being taken care of.

There are problems with homes for the aged. There are not enough homes, and people in general, do not want to go to them because they feel others will think their own family is failing in their obligation to take care of them. Also, the younger generation often do not want their parents to enter a home, because people will wonder why they cannot take care of their own parents. Even though there might be many problems with the older generation living with the younger, both sides usually prefer that the elder person does not live in a home for the aged.

Many older people go out and find some kind of work to do to support themselves. Sometimes they find a small room to rent, and are completely independent until they are very old. Only when they cannot take care of themselves at all, will they turn to their children for help. Today many people at seventy or eighty years of age still work. Their children must take care of their own children, and can give them only enough for the bare essentials of life. Therefore, they prefer to work in order to maintain a better standard of living.

The elderly people of Hong Kong have many problems. An old person has to be seventy years old to draw an old-age pension from the government and then it is only a token amount. It is not enough to feed a person, much less pay for other living expenses. They can also apply to the Welfare Department for additional support, and this is granted according to need. So, elderly people are quite dependent on the younger generation for support.

Babies

In Chinese traditional thinking, the more children a family has, the better. Children are a blessing, and are considered a form of wealth.

Chinese society is patriarchal, and throughout history Chinese have considered boys to be more important than girls. One reason is that boys carry on the family name. Also, when it comes time to divide up the family wealth, it is divided among males, of all generations. So, when a man's parents die, his portion of his parents' wealth will depend on the number of sons he has. For example, if he has no sons, his portion of the property will be less that his brother with three sons. Parents also depend on their sons for financial support in their old age.

There are many reasons why a couple wants
very much to have sons. In the past girls did not
go to school, nor did they go out to work. A
position in society was only for men, and it was
men who were eligible for the great honour of
positions in the government. So, a family would
encourage their sons to study and sit for government examinations. If they could pass and be
officials of the government, the family was very
honored and very happy.

During the feudal period, if a couple had been
married for two or three years and still did not
have children, the man's parents placed the blame
on the daughter-in-law. They would suggest that
the son take a concubine so he could have
children. If she did not have children, they would
find another one. It was acceptable to take several
concubines in order to have children, and especially sons. If children were born, but were female,
the man would continue to take other women in
order to try to have a son.

In the industrial society of Hong Kong it is
very expensive to raise children, and two children
per family has become quite popular. Even if the
first two are girls, most couples do not continue
to try for a boy. One reason is that today women
go out to work as much as men, so it is not
necessary to have boys for future financial
security. Still, many want very much to have a
son, and if they don't, they feel they are missing
something very important in life.

In the past, as soon as the family knew a wife was expecting, the women would begin to make clothes and shoes for the baby, as everything had to be made by hand. The expectant mother was not to do much work, but rest a lot and eat nourishing food. This was all done in great expectation of a son being born.

When the expectant mother started in labour, the mother-in-law would become very excited. She would prepare everything for the delivery. While the mother was in labour only the midwife, mother, and mother-in-law were allowed to enter the room. When the baby was born, everyone was very happy. If it was a boy they were all the more happy. They would run out to announce to all the family. If it was the first child, they would still be quite happy if it was a girl, assuring each other that the next one would be a boy.

It was usually the paternal grandfather, or perhaps grandmother, who chose the name for the child. Today, usually the parents choose the name for their child. Sometimes, to show respect for the elders, they might ask the grandparents to help choose a name.

A new mother must rest for the first month after the baby is born. She is only to take care of the baby, and get plenty of rest and sleep. However, if the mother or mother-in-law cannot help, or the family is not able to hire help, she might have to start doing her own housework sooner.

Until recent years the mother had no other choice than to breast feed her baby, so she had to eat very nourishing foods. A new mother must eat a special mixture of ginger, pigs' feet, and boiled eggs in vinegar, called *geung cho*, that is considered to be very nutritious and helpful in restoring normal health and strength. Two or three weeks before the baby is born the ginger is peeled and placed in the sun to dry. Then it is placed in a black, sweet vinegar and boiled. It is left in the vinegar, and reboiled every couple of days. When the baby is born, the pigs' feet are bought, cleaned thoroughly, boiled in water, and then put in with

the ginger and vinegar and boiled again. They must be boiled in water first, or the vinegar will cause the skin to toughen and become inedible. Then the eggs are boiled and peeled, and placed in the mixture. They are left until they become dark coloured, and then are ready to eat. Not only does the new mother, but the whole family eats it, and when friends and relatives come to visit the new baby and mother, it is served to them.

The mother must eat lots of chicken, and a soup made of fish and papaya. These are to cause her to produce lots of milk for the baby. Also, she is to drink some wine and several kinds of special nutritious teas, such as ginseng, to help her body gain back its strength.

It is thought that a mother should not take a bath or wash her hair for a time after having a baby. The period varies from two weeks to forty days, depending on the area of China a person is from. Many people think the mother should not take a bath for the first month or wash her hair for the first forty days. They think that the mother will be more susceptible to illnesses if she takes a bath too soon after giving birth. The peeling from the ginger used for the *geung cho* is saved and dried out, boiled in water with wine added, and is used by the mother for her first bath. This is thought to be especially good for killing germs. After this the mother can return to her normal habits of bathing daily. She may also start eating as usual; however, if the family can afford it, they might continue to provide special foods for her for at least another month.

The baby must be bathed daily, and fed when hungry. In the past people thought if a baby cried it needed to be fed. Today, people follow their doctor's instructions as to when to feed the baby. Most mothers bottle-feed their babies; for convenience as many mothers go out to work, and also because it is now not acceptable to breast-feed in public.

When people come to visit the mother and baby, they usually bring a gift. They might bring essence of chicken (in the past they would bring a pair of live chickens), eggs, or pigs' feet for the mother to eat. No gifts were given to the baby for the first month, though some families were accustomed to giving lucky money the first time they saw the baby. Today, gifts can be given to the mother or baby, or both, from the time it is born. Some people prefer to give lucky money.

When a baby is a month old, some families will give boiled eggs that have been dyed red (red represents a happy occasion), pickled ginger, and roast pork to friends and relatives to announce the baby's birth. Sometimes this is delivered to their homes. Other times they are given as they have occasion to see friends. For instance, sometimes they are brought to church meetings, or other functions, and passed out.

In general, when the baby reaches one month old, it is a time for celebration. Families who can afford it will have a big feast and invite all the friends and relatives to come. Family members and close friends might give gifts of gold or jade jewellery to the baby. Gifts of useful things, such as clothes, are also given. And, of course, lucky money can be given.

This custom of holding a feast to celebrate the child's month birthday is becoming less and less common. In a time when many new-born babies died, there was reason to celebrate when they reached a month old because the baby was past the critical stage. Today, because of the advance in medical technology, most babies live, and the real cause for celebration is no longer there. When a feast is held nowadays, most people only invite their immediate family members to the dinner. If the dinner is held in a restaurant, and the staff is told that the dinner is in celebration of the baby being a month old, the appetizer will be red eggs and pickled ginger. Everybody must eat one, as the egg represents new life.

Kai son or daughter

There seems to be no exact term in English to describe the custom Chinese people have of taking on a *kai* son or daughter. It seems to be very similar to "god child". However, for Chinese people it is a general custom, and not related to religion.

Taking on *kai* children is a very popular custom among Chinese people. Perhaps a couple has a son, but no daughter. If the couple has friends whose daughter they like very much, they might take the girl as their *kai* daughter. Or, vice versa, if they have daughters, and no sons.

Another situation might be that two couples who are very good friends might mutually decide to *kai* each others' children. The idea is that they will look after each others' children.

Sometimes there is superstition involved. A fortune teller will sometimes say a child's name is not good, and will bring bad luck to the parents. If they *kai* the child to another couple, then it will clear away any bad luck that the name might bring to the parents.

Also, if a couple has had a child who died at an early age, when their next child is born they will take it to a fortune teller, who will probably recommend that they find *kai* parents. This is to take away the bad luck, so that this child will not have the same fate as the previous child.

Many times taking on a *kai* son or daughter is done very casually, and there are no rights or obligations. The child will call the couple *kai* father and mother, and there will be a feeling of kinship between them, but nothing more.

However, sometimes a certain amount of ceremony is involved. A good date (Chinese have a custom of choosing auspicious days according to their almanac) is chosen. The *kai* parents will choose a gift for the child. This is a special day for the child, and he is not supposed to have to do any work. At the appointed time he will kneel before his *kai* parents, and serve tea to them. Then the couple will present a gift to the new *kai* child. This gift will be valuable; perhaps a piece of jade or gold jewellery. When a *kai* child is taken on in this way there are privileges and obligations involved. From time to time the couple will take the child out to eat with them or buy clothes or other things for him. They might take responsibility for extra things such as piano lessons, or, if necessary, all of his education expenses.

Then there are couples who have no children of their own, and like to take on *kai* children. The two families might have a feast and invite family and friends to formally announce that the one couple is taking the other couple's child as a *kai* child. The responsibilities of these *kai* parents are the same as those in the previous paragraph.

What privileges do the *kai* parents enjoy? When the child is grown up, if he is able, besides helping to provide for his own parents' needs, he will give some money to his *kai* parents each month to help them. If he cannot give money to them regularly, then he will give to them from time to time. There are times when the *kai* child will play the role of son or daughter to the *kai* parents. For instance, at the death of the *kai* parents he will help in making the arrangements for the funeral, just as a real son would do.

Adopting Children

In Chinese society, the adoption of children is not a common thing. It would be very unusual for a couple who already have children of their own to adopt other children.

If a couple has been married for a long time, perhaps seven or eight years, and still does not have children, they might consider adoption. Nowadays they would, of course, see a doctor first to find out for sure whether or not there is any possibility of their having children of their own. After they are quite sure they cannot, then they might consider adopting a son or daughter.

If a child is adopted, utmost effort will be made to keep it secret from the child. The adoptive parents will even try to keep the adoption a secret from friends and relatives. Of course, it is impossible to keep it from everyone, but those who know should never tell the child that these are not his natural parents. But, no matter how careful the parents are, there still might be an occasion when someone forgets and talks about the adoption in front of the child, or certain circumstances might arise under which the secret must be told.

The parents do not want the child to know that he is adopted because they are afraid he will not have proper filial respect for them when he grows up, or feel a duty to take care of them when they are old. They want him to have the same feelings

towards them as a natural child would towards
his parents. If the child knows he is adopted, and,
when he is grown, because of his own family
financial problems, he is unable to help support
his parents, they will feel it is because they are not
his natural parents. Likewise, the child will have
special problems with guilt feelings.

Also, if there are ever any problems with dis-
cipline or relations between the parents and the
child, people who know the child is adopted will
blame the problems on the fact that the child is
adopted. They might say things like, "Of course,
what can you expect, she didn't have the child
herself", or "If it were her own child, she wouldn't
punish him in that way." It can be seen that with
society's present thinking towards adoption, many
kinds of problems are involved with adoption.

In the past it was not necessary to register births
or get birth certificates for newborn babies. So
one couple would work out all the details with
another couple for adopting their child, without
having to go through any legal process.

In later years when the government started
requiring birth certificates, the adoptive parents
would take care of this matter after they got the
child. This was no problem, as babies were not
born in hospitals, but at home or in maternity
homes, and it was left up to parents to get birth
certificates. The midwife would write whatever
name she was instructed to on the birth papers.
The officials in the birth registry office paid no

attention to age of parents, and whoever applied for the birth certificate for a child could easily get it. The officials did not know nor care whether the child was adopted. So, as far as any legal records showed, the child was the couple's natural child.

Of course, this is not possible today. When a woman enters a hospital to have a baby she must show her identity card, then the baby is registered in the parents' names. A person must go through the proper legal channels to adopt a child.

Today if a couple wants to adopt a child they can go to an orphanage or to the government's Social Welfare Department. However, not many people want to go this route, as they want to know that it is from a good background. On the other hand, it is very difficult nowadays to privately adopt a child, as there are no private adoption agencies. Since satisfactory information cannot be obtained regarding children available for adoption, it is not very common to adopt children.

Chinese will never adopt a foreign child. The main reason is that because of the views of society towards adoption, they must try to keep it a secret, and if the child's skin, hair, and eyes are a different colour, it is impossible.

Birthdays

Chinese did not, traditionally, consider the anniversary of their birth as the day they become a year older, but New Year's Day. Also, they count the time from being conceived until being born as one year; so at birth they are already considered to be one year old. If they were born only ten days before the New Year, on New Year's Day they become two years old. This is the traditional way of figuring age; however, because most people nowadays get birth certificates when they are born, they are usually more accurate in giving their age.

It used to be very common practice for people to compare ages, and for a person to very casually ask another his age. However, in recent years people have become more secretive, and sometimes even young people will not tell their ages.

As to celebrating the birthday, children celebrate two especially. The first birthday is very important. Red eggs and long noodles must be prepared, along with many other foods. Red eggs represent life, and the long noodles represent long life. Even though the baby is not really old enough to eat these things, a little must be fed to him, as a symbol of good fortune. Many friends and relatives will be invited to celebrate this birthday with the family.

The next important birthday is the fifteenth. This is the time the child is considered to begin adulthood, and all the close friends and relatives will be invited. Buddhists have a custom of worshipping a certain idol for this special birthday. The child replaces all of his child-like clothing with more mature clothing, to represent the beginning of a new phase of his life.

Nowadays many families have adopted the Western practice of celebrating all of the children's birthdays. They buy a birthday cake, and usually invite only their cousins to come; however, the parents of the cousins usually come, too, since the children cannot come alone. They will have a birthday dinner together. Gifts will be brought for the child, usually toys. Since the toys usually do not cost much, they might also give lucky money. This dinner is usually in the home, not in a restaurant. Most families feel that to celebrate the children's birthdays every year is too much trouble, as everyone is so busy. Usually they celebrate a few, and then stop.

The next birthday of significance is the first one after marriage, and a big celebration will be held.

When a man is sixty, or a woman is sixty-one (some people like to wait until they are older, maybe seventy), they celebrate their "great age", *daaih sauh*. The sons and daughters will send out invitations, and many friends and relatives will be invited to a celebration feast.

If the family is Buddhist, on the morning of the celebration they will worship their ancestors.

In the past, on this day the daughters and daughters-in-law would dress up in the traditional Chinese dress. However, since these clothes are expensive, and seldom worn, today they usually just dress up in the modern style. They and the sons will serve tea to the parent and present their birthday gift, of money or gold, to him or her. The parent will, in return, give lucky money to the children when they serve the tea and give the gift. The amount of lucky money is irrelevant — it might be $5, up to $100. Besides lucky money, he will also give each child (or child-in-law) a gold peach pendant, as the peach symbolises long life. If he is not so well off financially he will only give one peach per family, but if he can afford it, he will give each person one.

After the tea ceremony, everyone will do as they please. In the past, in the afternoon friends and relatives would come to bring their regards. The friends would stay to play cards and mah-jong, and a caterer would be hired to come in to cook the birthday dinner. The sons and daughters would be there to care for the guests.

Nowadays, the dinner is usually held at a restaurant, and about 6 PM the family will go to the restaurant and be ready to greet the guests as they arrive. A big feast will be enjoyed together, and lots of pictures will be taken to commemorate the occasion. The feast will include red eggs and long noodles, and at the end of the meal sweet rolls will be served, which are in the shape of a peaches. These are all symbols for long life.

After the initial celebration of "great age", the person will begin celebrating his birthday each year. Only his immediate family members are invited; it will not be a big celebration like the first one.

In general, when an older person has a birthday, lucky money is given to him by children and close relatives. Also, the sons and daughters will go together in paying for the birthday feast.

Older people celebrate their birthdays according to the date of the lunar calendar. If the date falls on an inconvenient day when everyone is busy, they will change the celebration to another day, always before the actual date, never after. For instance, if a birthday falls on Tuesday it may be celebrated on the weekend before, never the weekend after. On the actual day a small family feast might also be held.

Funerals

Buddhist funerals

When a person dies the body is sent to a funeral home. The family chooses the date and time for the burial. The night before the burial the family gathers at the funeral home to decorate the funeral parlour. They hang a picture of the deceased person at the front of the hall, and the body is placed behind a curtain. On this night family members and friends begin to come to pay their last respects. The staff of the funeral home announce to the family when each guest arrives.

Then the guest will go to the front of the funeral
parlour, and the staff calls out for the guest to bow
to the deceased's picture a first, a second, and then
a third time. Then he calls for the family members
to bow to the guest. The guest is shown to a seat,
where he will then sit for awhile and visit with the
family members and try to comfort them. Things
like, "Don't be so broken-hearted", can be said,
or the guest can ask how the deceased's spouse or
other close family members are getting along. If
the guest had not heard that the person was ill, he
can take this opportunity to ask what the problem
was. After visiting with the family for awhile, the
guest may leave when he likes.

Buddhist monks will remain at the funeral
home all the time the family is there, and from
time to time they will chant the Buddhist scrip-
tures while they beat skull-shaped wooden drums.

The family will usually remain at the funeral
parlour from about 7 PM until midnight. In the
past, the family stayed the whole night, and did
not sleep at all, but nowadays the funeral parlour
closes, and does not allow them to stay all night.

On this night the family burns "hell money"
(imitation paper money made for this purpose),
incense, and candles to the deceased. The money
is for the deceased to use in Hades, candles are to
give them light, and the smoke from the incense
is considered as "rice", or the basic necessity for
the ghost of the dead person.

The family wears all white throughout the funeral rites. The women will also wear a white cloth around their head. White shoes and socks are also worn. The deceased's closest family members such as sons, daughters, daughters-in-law, and spouses will wear a piece of burlap on their heads. The more distant relatives, such as sons-in-law and grandchildren do not wear the burlap. The eldest son will wear a larger piece similar to a hat.

On the day of the burial, the family again puts on their funeral garments and returns to the funeral home. The time allowed for this is only about an hour. Friends and relatives come to show their respect and to share in the family's sorrow.

When attending a funeral, bright colours such as red, orange, or purple should never be worn. Close relatives and friends should be very careful to wear dull colours, such as grey, brown, or black, representing their sympathy for the family.

There are several things the guests can do to show their respect. The most usual thing is to buy a wreath of flowers. The guest can order a wreath from a shop near the funeral home, tell the shop clerk how much he wants to spend on it, who it is for and from, and the flower shop will deliver it to the funeral home right away. Also, gifts of blankets or suit fabric can be given. These are hung in the funeral hall with the deceased's name and the giver's name on them. However, some people feel that these things are not practical, and

will put money in a white envelope (never red, as
red is only for happy occasions) for the family to
use as needed. This usually is not a large amount
of money, maybe 101 or 201 dollars. It should
always be an uneven amount, as even numbers
represent good. On the outside of the envelope
the giver writes his name. This envelope is handed
to the person at the entrance of the funeral hall
who is in charge of registering the guests. This
person keeps a list of all gifts for the family, and
is usually a close friend, or distant relative, of
the family.

The person in charge of registering the guests
will then represent the family in giving something
in return to each guest. This is a white envelope
with red Chinese characters on it, which say
thank you. In the envelope is a handkerchief, a
piece of candy, and some money (usually a dol-
lar). The handkerchief is to wipe away tears of
sorrow, or when walking to the burial ground, to
wipe the perspiration. By eating the piece of
candy, all the bad "taste" of the death is taken
away, and good luck comes. The money is for bus
fare to return home, but most people do not use
it for that. As soon as they leave the funeral they
will buy more candy and eat it immediately. The
money is never carried home, as it is considered
unlucky money. As to the handkerchief, many
people think nothing of it, and will take it home
to use, but others consider it bad luck, and will
throw it away before reaching home.

There is a ceremony of putting the body in the casket. Actually, often the body is already placed in the casket, but the lid has not been closed. But, sometimes the body is resting on a bed, and at this time the casket is brought out and the body is placed in it. Then the whole family surrounds the casket and walks around it once while viewing the body. Then the staff of the funeral home place the lid on the casket and fasten it down.

A monk is invited to perform a ceremony to call the spirit out of the body before and after the body is placed in the casket. It is believed there are two places that the spirit might go to after death — heaven or hell. If a monk is not asked to call the spirit from the body, then the spirit will not be able to leave hell; the monk has the power to call the spirit out and get it into heaven. The family must pay money to the monk for this. The monk will then teach the family members all the appropriate rituals to perform to help the spirit.

After the ceremony, before the body is taken to the hearse, the oldest son must go out to "buy" water for the deceased. If the oldest son's wife is pregnant, he is not allowed to perform this task, and the next oldest son will be asked to do it. If there are no other sons, then a nephew or other close relative is chosen. He will take a small bucket to a faucet somewhere in the vicinity of the funeral home and draw some water. He "pays" for it by throwing down some hell money in the vicinity of where he drew the water. This symbolises buying water for the deceased to use in the after-life. Then, when he arrives there, the others will allow him to have water.

The casket is then taken to the hearse. The closest family members, the sons and spouse, for example, will ride in the hearse to the burial place. If there are family members who are quite old, some friends might be asked to take them home, as the trip would be too long and tiring for them.

Parents will attend the funeral ceremony, but will not go to the grave site for the burial ceremony of their children. It is considered that children are not worthy of receiving this show of respect from their parents. If the child is a small baby, then, of course, the parents will take care of the burial, because there is nobody else to do it.

Besides the hearse, any other family members might drive their own cars. If necessary, the family will provide a bus for all the family members and close friends to go to the grave site. (It is only family and very close friends who go to the grave site.) Those who ride in the hearse will throw out "hell money" along the way. This money is intended for those who have already died and gone to hell. It is to bribe them to treat this new one well who has come to join them. There is no set amount as to how much the family will throw out, they just continue until what they have brought is used up.

When the group arrives at the grave site there is a very simple ceremony. The grave has already been dug, and now the casket is put down in. The funeral home staff will ask the oldest son to check to be sure the casket is in the proper position. Then they ask if any family members have anything to place in the grave. They might have brought things that were dear to the deceased, such as clothing or household items. Then each member of the party will start the filling in of the grave by throwing in a handful of dirt. They will then burn candles, paper money, and paper clothing and shoes to the dead person, along with personal clothing that the deceased has worn, to be used where he now is. Then they leave.

When the burial service is over, the family, along with friends and relatives, go to a restaurant to eat. At the funeral service the time and place for the dinner will have been announced. If the funeral is in the morning, the dinner may be at noon or in the evening, whichever is more convenient. Or, they may go for tea at noon, and dinner in the evening. Usually, only the closest friends, relatives, and those who help the family with the funeral details attend the dinner. This dinner is not a big feast. There are seven courses served, as seven is the number for death.

After the family returns home they choose a place for a temporary altar, maybe the deceased's bedroom, or any place that is convenient to set up a table. On the wall above the table they hang the deceased's photograph. (This photograph is prepared after the death, and is hung up at the funeral home during the funeral, and on the hearse.) Candles, fresh flowers, incense, rice, wine, chopsticks, and fresh fruit are examples of what might be placed on the table. These are for the ghost of the deceased to eat and enjoy. The candles are lit and kept constantly burning. Incense is burned regularly by family members to show their respect. This goes on for at least seven days, though traditionally it was for seven weeks, but each family decides on the length of time. In the past is was often carried out for a whole year. After this period of time, the photograph of this deceased person will be placed with others at the family altar table, where candles and incense are burned regularly.

The family has a special wall, or even a room, if their home is large, where they will set up an altar permanently to hang the pictures of the deceased family members of two or three generations. Above this is a list of the deceased family members. Those who have died earlier are at the top, and this latest deceased is added at the bottom of the list. Then on special days they will light candles and burn incense, and place things such as rice, meat, and fresh fruit before them. This is done at least on the anniversary of the deceased's birthday, death, and the two special days each year for honoring the dead (Ching Ming and Chung Yeung Festivals).

Buddhists have a custom of a special ceremony on the seventh day after the funeral, and for each seventh day, up to seven weeks. The family members will burn paper money and candles to the deceased. Some families will make this a big occasion and will announce it to all family members and close friends. The people who join this event will first go to the home of the deceased to carry paper money and candles for the family to burn to the deceased; this is to show their respect to the deceased. They will stay and have a meal in the home, or go to a restaurant to eat together if the house is not big enough to accommodate so many people. Many families have modified this and only carry it out on the first and seventh weeks. Some compromise and carry it out on the first, third, and seventh weeks.

There is another custom common among Chinese people. Men and ladies wear a piece of black cloth, either pinned on their clothes or tucked in a pocket, to show there has been a death in the family. Or, the ladies will wear a flower, made of yarn, in their hair. These flowers are several colours — white, blue, green, and red. White represents the closest of kin, such as husband, parents, or parents-in-law. In the past these were worn for three years. They would wear white for one year, and then change to blue and wear it for two years. But now it has become much more simplified. Many people are superstitious and do not like to see people wear the cloth or flowers, and especially would not welcome them into their homes. If a special occasion is held during the time when the flower or cloth is being worn, the wearer will definitely not attend.

For the shorter period of wearing the symbols for one year, white is worn for the first three months, and then changed to blue. Some have reduced it even more, and wear it for only 100 days. For the first seven weeks white is worn and then changed for blue. Each family decides how long to wear the symbols. Some families will shorten it even more, for particular reasons. For instance, if New Year is close they might only wear it for seven weeks. They would not want to wear it during the New Year, as it would make them sad, and, after all, the living are more important.

The colours of the flowers represent the relation to the deceased. White is for the closest of kin. The next generation, grandchildren, wears blue. More distant relatives, such as nieces, wear green. Those who wear green only wear it for a few days, and then they change to red, which is worn for only one or two days. Red represents a happy occasion, and means that it is the end of mourning.

There are two kinds of caskets available — Chinese and Western. The Chinese style is more simple, made of boards which curve out at the end. Western style is more ornate. It is up to the family of the deceased to choose the style. Many people think the wood of the Chinese style is better and will last longer.

As to burial or cremation, at least ninety percent of Chinese people will prefer burial. They feel that to enter the ground is natural. But due to the shortage of grave sites in crowded Hong Kong, it is very difficult and expensive to obtain a permanent burial place, and cremation is becoming more common. The situation in Hong Kong now is that, no matter if it is a government, Christian, or other private graveyard, the space is usually only rented. After five or seven years the bones are dug up and the space is then used by another person.

Within a few months after the burial the family will have a memorial stone erected over the grave. This makes the grave much neater and easier to keep clean, and makes it much more convenient for worship. Also, it provides a place for family members, when visiting, to sit and rest.

After seven years of burial, the bones must be dug up. The bones may then be put in a big jug, and a spot of ground found on which to place it. Or, the bones may be cremated after they are dug up. The remains might be placed in the rack at the cemetery along with others. If the family is Taoist or Buddhist they might take the remains and place them in the ancestral hall of a temple. The reason for this is so the monks or nuns can burn candles and incense for them, and place fruit before them.

Sometimes a family will choose a burial plot near a temple. Then, for instance, all the Ngs will be buried in the same place. They will then buy a space in the nearby temple, where the pictures and particulars of the deceased will then be posted, so that people will know who is buried in the area. Sometimes when a husband or wife dies, the family may wish to reserve a space beside the spouse for the mate, and buy both spaces at the same time. The spouse's picture may also be placed alongside the deceased's, with a red piece of paper stuck to the bottom of the space to show that this person is still living.

After a cremation service, the ashes are placed in a jug that can be bought for this purpose. The cemeteries (both government and Christian) have special racks for the purpose of storing the ashes. On the outside is a place for a picture and the particulars of the deceased. There is also a small shelf on which fresh flowers may be placed. Family members will go there for worshipping the ghost of the deceased on Ching Ming and Chung Yeung festivals. Worship consists of burning incense and carrying flowers and foods for the ghost to enjoy.

Christian funerals

In general, a Christian funeral follows the same pattern of Christian funerals in Western countries. Because of the long history of Buddhism in China, many of the Buddhist customs have become a part of Chinese culture, just as in some Western countries Christian customs have become a part of Western culture. Therefore, at Christian funerals, many Buddhist customs are seen, such as the gifts and the symbols worn to signify the death of a family member.

However, there are some noticeable differences. At a Christian funeral the family members wear black robes, not white. It might be said that this is just Western custom, and not Christian. This might be true, but, nevertheless, it has become one of the distinguishing factors between the Buddhist and Christian funeral.

Most families will give out the white packets to the guests; but there are some families who consider this superstitious, and will not give them.

Also, some Christians do not bow to the deceased, or to their picture. Usually, when a person enters the funeral hall they will go to the front and stand for a moment looking at the picture of the deceased as a means of showing their respect. However, even this is not mandatory, and some people enter the funeral hall and go directly to a seat.

The custom of giving gifts of flowers, money, blankets, or suit material is also practiced among Christians, and is carried out in the same manner as in Buddhism.

Other titles
from
Asia 2000

Non-fiction

Fiction

Photo Books

Order from Asia 2000 Ltd
1101–02 Seabird House, 22–28 Wyndham St
Central, Hong Kong
tel (852) 2530 1409; fax (852) 2526 1107